RICHARD W. SKINNER

FOREWORD

A portrait of Oblt. Z. See Hans-Gert Mahrholz. (By kind permission of Hans-Gert Mahrholz).

It is not easy for me to find the right words for this book, but I wish to try in memory of my former crew members of U-309 who lost their lives in the last months of the Second World War.

I was the first commander of U-309, and put it into service on the 27th January 1943 at the 'Flenderwerk' in Lübeck. After the usual and very intensive period of instruction, we went on our first operational mission, on the 26th August 1943, to the North Sea. Further missions followed from our home-base at Brest, including Atlantic patrols.

During the instruction period in the Eastern Sea the crew had developed into a really good and ideal team. Each man on board knew his tasks or duties, and acted automatically. I always felt safe being with these men on operational patrols, especially in this most difficult period of the U-boat war. At the end of our last and very difficult patrol, to the invasion front in the English Channel, we rescued most of the crew of U-981 (Commander Keller).

On return I handed my boat over to Oblt. Z. See Herbert Loeder at La Rochelle. He took the U-309 back to Germany for a shipyard time-out and general inspection, before departing on an operational patrol. The war was almost at it's end when U-309 found her destiny and was sunk with her entire crew in the Moray Firth. It was February the 16th 1945.

The memories of the events of this time, even after the decades that have since passed, still fill me with mourning and pain.

Hans-Gert Mahrholz,
Fregattenkapitän a. D. (Ret'd.)
Germany, 9th November 2002.

U-309

The Officers and crew of U-309 on the 27th January 1943 - the day she was commissioned. The symbol on the port side of the conning tower, two white bars above a white downward facing triangle, is a 'UAK' symbol. The 'UAK' symbol was shown on both sides of a U-boat's conning tower until the boat was accepted into the Kriegsmarine by the U-boat Acceptance Command. Each construction yard had it's own symbol configuration, and this example is that of Flenderwerft at Lübeck. (By kind permission of the U-boat Archive).

U-309 was a fighting unit of wartime Germany's Kriegsmarine - one of the many U-boats that served during the Second World War. She was built in Lübeck by Flenderwerft, with her keel laid on the 21st January 1942. The boat was launched on the 14th December 1942 and she was commissioned into the German Navy on the 27th January 1943, with the Feldpost number M49 703. Her first commander was Oberleutnant Hans-Gert Mahrholz, who was onboard from January 1943 until August 1944.

During its service, U-309 carried out 8 patrols. The boat damaged one vessel and sank none.

U-309's service started in January 1943 with the 8th training flotilla, which was based at Danzig, on the Baltic coast. This training period ended in July of that year when U-309 left Danzig for Kiel. Courtesy of the allies' ability to decode German Enigma traffic, some of U-309s activity was known to the British[1]. On the 18th February 1943, for example, the Officer in Charge of the West Baltic Coast signaled the Warnemuende Guardship that U-309 had left Kiel for Danzig. The next day, U-309 herself sent a message to Danzig indicating that she expected to arrive there at 15.00 hours on the following Friday, and that accommodation was required for her crew.

Another shot of some of the crew of U-309 on her commissioning day. It is unfortunately not recorded who the reviewing officer was. The three men on the right have collar patches indicating that they are Petty Officers. The two left hand of these Petty Officers are wearing the U-boat badge, suggesting that they are veterans of other U-boats. The third is wearing the Minesweepers War Badge which indicates that he served on an anti-submarine or other escort vessel prior to entering the U-boat service and joining U-309. Introduced in 1940, this badge was awarded for completion of three operational patrols. (By kind permission of the U-boat Archive).

On the 26th August 1943, she left Kiel for the Norwegian port of Bergen, where she arrived on the 1st September 1943. Bergen was the home port of the 11th U-boat flotilla, of which U-309 was now an operational unit. Almost two weeks later she sailed further north to Trondheim where her first operational patrol would begin on the 25th September under the command of Oberleutnant Mahrholz. U-309 joined the 'Rossbach' Group to the south and west of Iceland where they would search for eastbound convoys. During this period, crewman Erich Jungmann, aged 19 years, was swept overboard and lost whilst the boat was operating in the North Atlantic. Having no success the group moved south on the 5th October forming a new patrol line in order to search for convoys HX259 and SC143.

On the 7th October convoy SC143 was presumed to be in the area, but when a reconnaissance aircraft sighted the convoy on the 8th, its homing signals were not received by the hunting wolfpack. The allies stepped up patrols during the day and three boats, U-610, U-643 and U-419, were all sunk. U-610 went to the bottom of the Atlantic with all her crew. The 'Rossbach' operation was called off on the morning of the 9th October.

Southeast of Greenland a new group named 'Schlieffen' was being formed, and U-309 was ordered to join it and help in the search for 'ONS20' - a westbound convoy. This instruction was passed to U-309 on the 13th October, and followed on the 17th by a further warning that a convoy was in square AK 3558[2]. On the same day, all other

The personal emblem of U-309. This shows a sparrow standing on a periscope protruding from the waves, and earned U-309 the nickname 'U-Spatz' or 'U-Sparrow'. Divers that have visited the wreck site state that the remains of this emblem and its plaque can still be seen bolted to the front of the conning tower. (By kind permission of the U-boat Archive).

'Schlieffen' boats were ordered to "get at Mahrholz's convoy". The group moved northwards on the 14th, but late on the 15th U-844, which was outward bound on patrol sighted a different westbound convoy - 'ON206'.

U-844 was ordered to maintain contact and wait for the arrival of U-309 and the 'Schlieffen' group. However, the next day the boat was located and sunk with all hands by allied aircraft southwest of Iceland. The Iceland based aircraft were proving so successful in keeping the 'Schlieffen' group below the surface, that it was becoming increasingly difficult to locate the convoy. Moving further eastwards, the group formed a new, more concentrated patrol line on the 17th October 1943. That morning the convoy 'ONS20' passed just north of the new patrol

The conning tower of U-309 whilst she was in either Brest or Bordeaux. The presence of the 'laughing swordfish' emblem dates the picture between November 1943 and October 1944. This emblem was that of the 9th Flotilla, whose headquarters was at Brest. The Officer in the white cap, standing in the middle of the picture, is OL. Hans-Gert Mahrholz. Also worthy of note is the plaque mounted on the front of the conning tower which carries the personal badge of U-309. (By kind permission of the U-boat Archive).

line and the boats were ordered to attack. U-309 fired a spread of four torpedoes. These obviously missed, as all that her crew heard were the end of run explosions. Later that day all contact with convoy 'ONS20' was lost when the merchantmen altered course. Continuing searches for the convoy were halted on the evening of the 17th and the 'Schlieffen' group moved west to avoid continued harassment by allied aircraft. At noon on the 18th the operation ended.

With six boats lost, the survivors of the 'Schlieffen' group were joined by new arrivals to form the 'Siegfried' group. On the 22nd October 1943, Mahrholz signaled that he was in place with the 'Siegfried' group. By the 24th October U-309 and the new group were some 500 miles east of Newfoundland. Days later Mahrholz and his crew would leave the group and sail for their new base on the French Atlantic Coast at Brest, home of the 9th U-flotilla.

The Captain U-boats West transmitted this move to U-309 on the 29th October at 15.13 hours. In the same message, U-214 was instructed to make for Lorient. U-309 duly sailed into the French port on the 11th November 1943.

Oberleutnant Hans-Gert Mahrholz and his crew spent over a month in Brest until, on the 19th December, U-309 departed on patrol with orders to operate in an area west of the British Isles. It was planned to have U-309 join the 'Rügen' groups, of which there were six. The boats in these groups were very dispersed, being five groups of three, and one

Top: A view, looking forward, of the late war version conning tower on U-309.
Middle: Crew member from U-309 being awarded his Iron Cross by Kapitän zur See Roesing. The date is the 10th November 1943.
Bottom: Oblt. Z. See Hans-Gert Mahrholz at the same ceremony receiving his Iron Cross. In the background, part of the buildings of the 9th U-Flotilla Headquarters at Brest, can be seen.
(All by kind permission of Hans-Gert Mahrholz).

Top: One of the original crew members of U-309 who served under Mahrholz. This is WO.I. Erhard Wendelberger.
Middle: A photograph of another original crew member. Moments later his head would be shaved completely bald for having lost a bet!
Bottom: U-309 heads out to sea in late 1943. Note the guide ship in the distance.
(All by kind permission of Hans-Gert Mahrholz).

group of four. The intention was to give the allies the impression, that whilst constantly changing position, a greater number of boats were operating over a wide area. However, this idea backfired on the German high command. When a convoy was found, the groups of U-boats were too small to carry out any successful attacks and subsequently the 'Rügen' groups were dispersed on the 7th January 1944. These boats, including U-309 were now to operate as single fighting units in their own specified areas.

It was not only vital military information that the allies gathered through the work of the Enigma decoders. At 13.26 hours on the 6th January 1944 operators intercepted a message of a more personal nature[3]. This message was addressed to 24 year old Kurt Feller onboard U-309. It read simply: "Son and heir arrived. Mother and child well. Anton". The 9th U-boat flotilla added a single word - "Congratulations"[4].

On the 26th January 1944, the 'Stürmer' group was formed, comprising of U-309 and other ex-'Rügen' boats. Mahrholz confirmed this in a message sent the same day at 21.22 hours. To the northwest of the North Channel they awaited the arrival of convoy ON221, which had been sighted by German reconnaissance aircraft on the 27th. Unfortunately for the Germans, the aircraft was experiencing technical difficulties and was unable to home in on the U-boats group, including U-309. Despite exhaustive searches being made throughout the 28th, the convoy was not found. Following a report by an aircraft on the 29th, that an invasion of

Western France was expected, the operation was terminated. All boats operating in the North Atlantic, including the 'Stürmer' group, were ordered to make for the Biscay Coast at high speed. Soon after, it became apparent that the 'invasion fleet' was in fact a group of Spanish trawlers and all boats were ordered to return to their operational areas.

On the 31st January 1944, the 'Stürmer' group was once more on station northwest of the North Channel. In this period there was a noticeable increase in the allied anti-submarine defences, and U-309 along with the 'Stürmer' group slowly withdrew further westwards. On the 14th February U-309 arrived at Bordeaux, and on April 8th the boat left Bordeaux bound for La Pallice, where she arrived two days later.

On the 20th June 1944, U-309 left La Pallice bound for Cherbourg. The purpose of this voyage was to transport artillery and small arms ammunition to the port, which had been cut-off by the allies. On the 23rd, the operation was cancelled when it was discovered that the harbour entrance to Cherbourg had been blocked. U-309 returned to Brest on the 25th June, arriving at 08.15 hours. A few days later the boat left on patrol for operations in the English Channel, her Enigma traffic indicating that she left Brest at 22.30 hours on the 29th. Whilst on route to the area, U-309 was recalled, and instructed to wait until allied activity in the invasion area became less frequent. Whilst on her return voyage, U-309 made an unsuccessful attack on a destroyer southwest of Bolt Head.

Top: One of the crew of U-309 during one of the early patrols. Note the 'sparrow' emblem on his forage cap.
Middle: The same emblem can be seen on the front of the conning tower, along with the 9th U-Flotilla insignia, in this shot of U-309 at sea in late 1943.
Bottom: Mahrholz, in the white cap, on return from a patrol in early 1944. Next to him is the Knights Cross winner Scholz.
(All by kind permission of Hans-Gert Mahrholz).

Mahrholz and his crew arrived at Brest on the 6th July 1944. Six days later on the 12th, U-309 left the shelter of the massive U-boat bunker in Brest and sailed for operations, again in the English Channel. She reached the area on the 19th and on the 20th unsuccessfully attacked a ship in a convoy to the south of the Isle of Wight. On the 24th July U-309 torpedoed and damaged the *S.S. Samneva*[5] a merchantman of over 7,000 tons, northeast of Barfleur, before returning to Brest on the 3rd August 1944.

As the allies closed in and surrounded the northern Biscay ports, U-309 left Brest for the last time on the 7th July 1944. Accompanied by other boats on the 12th, and whilst U-309 and U-981 were approaching a rendezvous point off La Pallice, U-981 struck a mine. With U-981 unable to move or dive, U-309 stopped to assist. Two hours later both boats were detected on the surface by a Halifax II aircraft of No.502 Squadron RAF.

With insufficient room to prepare a bombing run, the aircraft dropped three flares. Frantically the crew of U-981 managed to restart their electric motors and both U-boats moved slow ahead, 100 yards apart. After dropping more flares, the Halifax finally approached at 7,300 feet and released five 600lb bombs. The rear gunner on the Halifax saw four bombs burst around U-981, which started to make tight turns to port[6]. Approximately twenty minutes later with the Halifax moving away, the crew of U-981 proceeded to abandon ship[7]. At 06.43 hours,

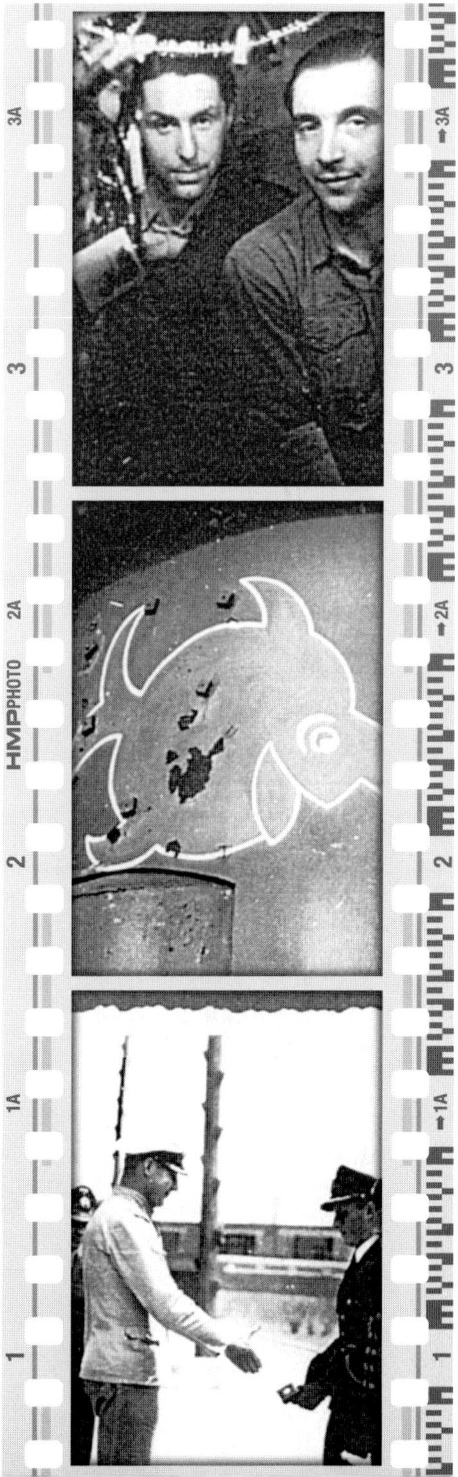

Top: Crew members of U-309 enjoy the Christmas of 1943 on board ship, with a few Christmas lights and decorations reminding them of more peaceful times.
Middle: A side on view of the conning tower of U-309 illustrating the 'laughing swordfish' emblem of the 9th U-Flotilla.
Bottom: Following another successful patrol a crew member from U-309 is congratulated by Kapitän Leutnant Willenbrock. Dressed in white, and a holder of the Knights Cross, Willenbrock was the commander of the 9th U-Flotilla.
(All by kind permission of Hans-Gert Mahrholz).

whilst U-981 plunged to the bottom of the Gironde Estuary, U-309 closed in and picked up forty survivors of its crew. In the attack, one officer and eleven crewmen lost their lives. Heavily laden, U-309 sailed into La Pallice later the same day.

Above: The two page entry in the Guest Book of the 5th U-Flotilla relating to U-309. Drawn by a crew member of U-309, the basis of the sketch is the letter 'M' from the first Commander's nickname 'Matz'. The signatures on the right hand side are, from top to bottom, those of Mahrholz himself; Lt. (Eng) Platzek; WO.I. Wendelberger; and WO.II. Leopold. (By kind permission of the U-boat Archive).

Below: The ability of the allies to decode and read the German Navy's Enigma transmissions had a profound effect on the course of the Second World War. Here is one of the encoded Enigma messages that relates to U-309. The date and time of the message can be seen top right - 20.18 hours on the evening of the 30th January 1945. Both of the U-boats named on the message - U-878 and U-309 would not see the end of the war. The U-878 was sunk in the Atlantic, by H.M.S. *Vanquisher* and H.M.S. *Tintagel Castle*, on the 10th April 1945. (By kind permission of the Public Record Office. Reference HW 18/406, page 41).

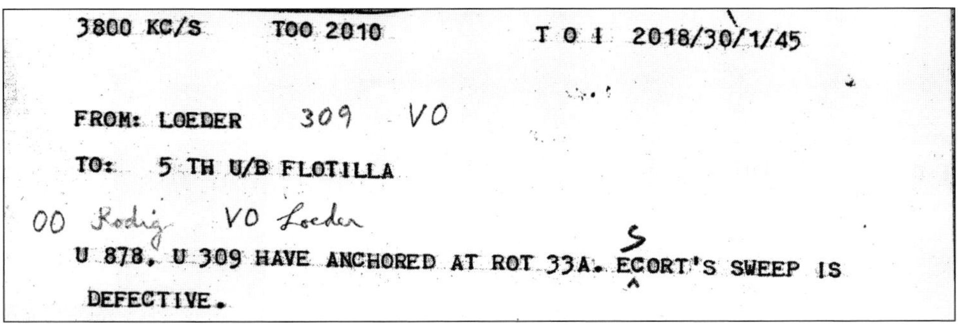

3800 KC/S TOO 2010 T O I 2018/30/1/45

FROM: LOEDER 309 VO

TO: 5 TH U/B FLOTILLA

OO Rodig VO Loeder

U 878, U 309 HAVE ANCHORED AT ROT 33A. ECORT'S SWEEP IS DEFECTIVE.

A NEW COMMANDER

During the month of August 1944, U-309 became the new command of Oberleutnant Herbert Loeder. This would be the 25-year-old officer's first and last command. The former commander, Mahrholz, was destined for the 1st Radar Training Branch and would be the more fortunate of the two in that he was to survive the war.

On the 29th August, U-309 and her new commander sailed for operations in British coastal waters. She had set out for the North Channel, but because of the strong allied anti-submarine activities, the submarine was unable to reach her operational area. All the French Biscay bases had now been evacuated, so U-309 set course for Norway and arrived at Stavanger on the 13th October 1944.

Between October 1944 and January 1945, U-309 sailed from Norway and arrived in Germany. The boat was now an operational unit of the 33rd Flotilla, which had its base at Flensburg in the far north of Germany. On the 30th January 1945, U-309 left Kiel. She arrived at Horten, Norway, on the 2nd February.

On the 8th, U-309, her commander Oberleutnant Herbert Loeder and his crew bade farewell to their comrades in Norway and left on their final patrol. The boat now sailed for British coastal waters and eventually reached her operational zone - the Moray Firth, off the north-east coast of Scotland. Once again the historian can learn a little of the U-309 activities from decoded Enigma transmissions. On the 10th February, Loeder reported making changes in his course near Kristiansand because of problems with fog[1]. On the 15th, he was ordered by the Captain U-boats West to tune radios to the 'Diana' settings.

The second Commander of U-309 - Oberleutnant Herbert Loeder. Born on the 3rd April 1919, Loeder was lost with the remainder of the crew of U-309. The star insignia on his left arm indicates that he was a line officer - Seaman Branch. (By kind permission of the U-boat Archive).

At the same time that U-309 was manoeuvring herself into position to obey these instructions, two other 'factors' were moving towards her - two factors that would ultimately seal her fate. The first of these was convoy WN.74. This convoy, consisting of 7 vessels, weighed anchor at Loch Ewe at 19.00 on the 15th February, and was heading south for a number of different destinations[2]. Three vessels in the convoy were bound for Hull -

The H.M.C.S. *Saint John* at sea on the 15th November 1944. By February 1945 the *Saint John*, along with other members of Escort Group 9, had already become an accomplished 'sub hunter'. On the 1st September she attacked a contact in the English Channel. Evidence gathered at the time, including a certificate celebrating the victim's ten millionth engine revolution, indicated that it had been U-247. (By kind permission of the family of the late Cable Freeman).

the Norwegian *Berhard* (on which the Commodore was travelling); the Danish *Norco* (carrying the Vice-Commodore); and the Icelandic *Selfoss*. The other Norwegian vessel in the convoy, the *Harpefjell*, was on route to Grangemouth; whilst H.M.Y. *Skyrack* was headed for Southend; the H.M.S. *Saltburn* to Leith; and H.M.T. *Marie Louise* was bound for Aberdeen. Maintaining an average speed of 8.2 knots the convoy was under the protection of two trawlers - H.M.T.s *Stoke City* and *Polka*.

Even at this late stage of the war, the Admiralty was aware that the U-boat threat was still present. In the instructions for the passage of WN.74, it was noted that "it is evident that the enemy now intends to carry U-boat warfare into coastal waters both at home and abroad. Masters are therefore warned a) to ensure that no relaxation of vigilance and safety measures occur until their ship is in harbour, and b) that every endeavour is to be made to remain in close formation in coastal waters in order to afford escorts a better opportunity for protection of the convoy"[3].

The Commodore reported that the convoy encountered no problems in its passage. Indeed he noted that station keeping and signalling were good, and that the vessels were able to maintain the required speed for the convoy.

In his report Commodore Tweedie does not give an indication that he was aware that his presence might have caused the loss of a U-boat. WN.74 itself did not encounter U-309, but its presence off this stretch of Scottish coast drew the second 'factor' into the story. The 9th Escort Group, and in particular H.M.C.S *Saint John*, had been ordered to head towards, and monitor, WN.74. It was, as we shall see, the presence of the warships in this group that would ultimately lead to the sinking of U-309.

The 9th Escort Group, EG-9, was based at Londonderry, Northern Ireland, and served under the control of the Western Approaches Command. EG-9 was, on paper, a force of seven frigates, though through repairs, damage, modifications, leave and other operational demands, it was rare for all members of the force to be operational at the same time. H.M.C.S. *Saint John* had joined EG-9 in May 1944, and in the summer of that year Commander A.F.C. Layard DSO selected the *Saint John* to be EG-9's senior officer's ship.[4]

During the dark days of the Battle of the Atlantic it was the corvette that had formed the basis of the Royal Canadian Navy's war at sea. Despite having been designed primarily as a coastal escort vessel, the corvettes soon found themselves operating in the more hazardous deep-sea service. This over-extension of the capabilities of the corvette class was soon recognised, and a new twin-screw vessel, 96-foot longer than the Flower class corvettes, proposed. When these plans were first shown in Canada Vice-Admiral Percy Nelles, Chief of the Canadian Naval Staff, suggested the class name 'Frigate'. Orders followed straight away - 60 for the Canadian Navy and a further 10 for the British.

Laid down on the 28th May 1943, H.M.C.S. *Saint John* was one of these new frigates from the 1942-43 programme of 'River' class vessels.[5] Built by Canadian Vickers Ltd of Montreal, Quebec, the *Saint John* was launched on the 25th August 1943 and commissioned, with the pennant number K456, on the 13th December that year. Her

A view of the conning tower of U-309 clearly showing the 9th Flotilla insignia and her own 'sparrow' emblem. Mahrholz can be seen wearing the white cap. (By kind permission of Hans-Gert Mahrholz).

Photographed from the *Saint John*, vessels from E.G.9 are pictured in line astern. (By kind permission the family of the late A.J. Clarke).

new twin screw design allowed a top speed of 19 knots and, together with the increased size (301 foot long and a displacement of 1445 tonnes), she was capable of a maximum range of 7,200 miles. The River class design also saw improvements in armament - the *Saint John* mounted a 4" main gun, powered twin-mount Oerlikons and a considerably larger load of ammunition - including no less than 200 depth charges. To function, the *Saint John* required a crew of 8 officers and 133 ratings.[6]

As 1944 passed into 1945, EG-9 was kept busy, so much so that H.M.C.S. *Saint John* and her cohorts were almost permanently at sea. By now, the *Saint John* was already an accomplished 'sub-chaser' for on the 1st September 1944 she had sunk U-247 during an anti-submarine sweep off Land's End.[7] Earlier that year, in a report dated the 27th April 1944, Rear Admiral L.W. Murray R.C.N., the Commander-in-Chief of the Canadian Northwest Atlantic, penned his thoughts on the work of the *Saint John*. Commenting on her abilities to the Captain of the *Saint John* he wrote, somewhat prophetically, that "it augurs well for the future and ill for any U-boat you may come across!".

In November she and other frigates from EG-9, the *Monnow, Nene, Port Colbourne, Stormont* and *Loch Alvie,* escorted Convoy JW-62 to the Kola Inlet in Russia, returning a month later to Loch Ewe with RA-62. By January 1945 EG-9 was operating off the Cornish Coast, and then in February they headed north to the Orkneys and the north coast of Scotland. Hardly had they arrived when, on the morning of the 16th February, the *Saint John*, patrolling the Pentland Firth in company with *Nene, Loch Alvie* and *Monnow* was instructed to support Convoy WN-74.[8] U-309 and the *Saint John* had been placed on a collision course that, for the former, would have disastrous consequences.

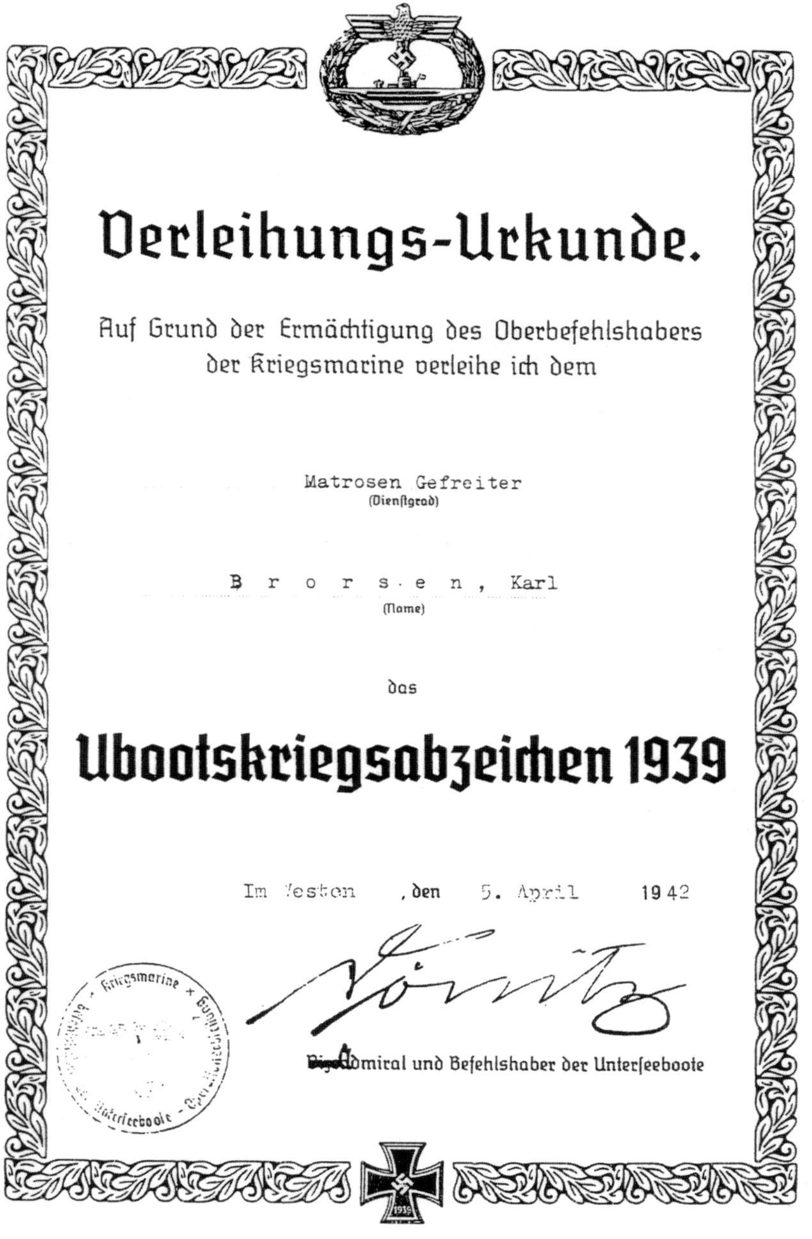

Verleihungs-Urkunde.

Auf Grund der Ermächtigung des Oberbefehlshabers der Kriegsmarine verleihe ich dem

Matrosen Gefreiter
(Dienstgrad)

B r o r s e n , Karl
(Name)

das

Ubootskriegsabzeichen 1939

Im Westen , den 5. April 1942

Admiral und Befehlshaber der Unterseeboote

The certificate awarded to all German submariners who qualified for the U-boat War Badge or *Ubootkriegsabzeichnen.* To be awarded this, a seaman had to complete two war patrols aboard a frontline U-boat. Such requirements could, however, be waived by a Commanding Officer for feats of exceptional service or outstanding bravery. This particular certificate was awarded to Matrosen Gefreiter Karl-Heinz Brorsen. Brorsen, born on the 16th March 1921, was one of those lost in the sinking of U-309. Of particular interest is the fact that this certificate bares the signature of Gross Admiral Donitz. (By kind permission of the U-boat Archive).

THE ATTACK

The bow of the *Saint John*, pictured from the bridge. Note the forward 4″ gun. (By kind permission of the family of the late A.J. Clarke).

At 04.05 hours on the morning of Friday the 16th February 1945 the radar operators on H.M.C.S. *Saint John* reported that they had established radar contact with Convoy WN.74.[1] Over the next two hours the frigates of EG-9 followed an indirect zig-zagging course that saw the *Monnow* and *Loch Alvie* take station on the port quarter of WN.74 and *Saint John* and *Nene* astern on the starboard side.[2] Routine duties and watch changes continued unabated in the ships of EG.9 as the merchantmen ploughed onwards, passing Pentland Firth at 10.05 hours.

Throughout the morning a flooding tide caused the convoy to get slightly off track, so Commodore Tweedie instructed that a course of 146° be set in an attempt to regain the convoy lane. Due to intermittent fog, the vessels of EG-9 failed to notice this change, and a subsequent one to 110°, and so eventually found themselves steaming off to the starboard wing of the convoy. At this point, the ships were using independent zig-zag courses of approximately 50° on each side of the main course and as the *Saint John* turned to a starboard 'zag' a contact was gained on a bearing 245° at 900 yards.[3]

It was at 14.35 hours that the Asdic operator, Able Seaman Norman Hoffner, of Turner Valley, Alta., reported that he had detected the presence of what he believed was a U-boat. What followed was, according to the Officer of the Watch at the time, Lieutenant James Bradley R.C.N.V.R., an example of "perfect co-ordination between Asdic operators, depth charge parties and the bridge".[4] There was neither doppler nor movement, and so a run was made over the target at 14.45 in an attempt to obtain an echo-sounder trace and QH fix. The echo-sounder showed a bottomed contact, whilst the latter indicated a contact that was well clear of all charted 'non-subs' in the vicinity.[5] In fact, the echo-sounder provided the crew of *Saint John* with evidence that the object was approximately 130ft by 16ft in size - which, as previous experience had shown, was almost certainly an enemy U-boat.[6]

The *Saint John* commenced her attack at 14.55 hours with a five-charge pattern of heavy depth charges set to explode at 225 feet. The immediate results were a large flow of oil and small pieces of softwood painted grey. Could the crew of U-309 be trying to throw the *Saint John* off the scent, or had the fatal blow just been struck? Undaunted, the *Saint John* continued with, at 15.30, Hedgehog bringing more oil and wood to the surface.[7] During this time several other echo-sounder runs had been made and further evidence gathered that suggested it was a U-boat that was under attack.

At 15.55 another five-charge pattern of depth charges were fired. These depth charges were fired according to the system that the crew of *Saint John* had worked out themselves, and which had been used to startling effect in the sinking of U-247.[8] Further wreckage began to bubble to the surface, and at 16.40 the Captain of the *Saint John* ordered the sea boat away in an attempt to gather evidence of a possible victory.[9] Amongst the fragments pulled from the water were a German signal pad, a dented canteen that smelled of liquor,

The H.M.C.S. *Saint John* tied up at her home port of Saint John in the summer of 1945. Her pennant number of K-456 can be clearly seen. (By kind permission of Market Square, Saint John).

Above: The crew of the *Saint John* at action stations on the bridge. The ship is off the North coast of Scotland.

Opposite: Depth charges detonating in the wake of H.M.C.S. *Saint John*. The target of these explosions is believed to be U-309. (Both photographs by kind permission of the family of the late A.J. Clarke).

a tube of boracic acid that was marked 'Medical Stores Kiel', and yet more pieces of the grey, soft, freshly splintered wood.

A large radio tube with wire hanging from it, appearing as though it had been torn loose, was seen floating by. It remained out of reach of the sea boats' crew retrieving the wreckage by means of a small net. A sample of the oil was also collected, and later found to be diesel oil of a type used by the German navy.

With the sea boat back on board, the *Saint John* once more got under way and resumed her attack. At 17.14 a further five depth charges were fired, followed by another ten at 17.35. Still more oil, including what appeared to be lubricating oil, and splintered wood fragments were brought to the surface. At 18.00 a Hedgehog barrage was plotted by the echo sounder straddling the object that was still bottomed on the seabed. This brought forth another tremendous flow of oil. Two more attacks were carried out before dark - five depth charges at 18.30 and a pattern of ten more at 19.00. In all cases, the attacks were broken off if the echo sounder did not show that the target was being crossed.

Commander Layard, Royal Navy Senior Officer of EG.9, then signaled to H.M.C.S. *Nene* that she was to detach from WN.74 and assist in the attack.[10] Almost immediately though, it was found that the presence of two frigates was causing problems with the Asdic readings and *Nene* was ordered to pull back and take station three miles from the target. It was decided that, with night falling, the *Saint John* would monitor and hold the contact till the morning, circling 1,000 to 1,500 yards from its location. Through the hours of darkness, her crew re-examined the many echo sounder traces and a more definite location of the target established. Two further traces were made at 06.10 and 06.30 on the morning of the 17th to assure that the contact had not moved. The submarine still lay where she had first been

The Quarter Deck of the *Saint John* awash in a heavy sea. Note the presence of the depth charges and the launchers. (By kind permission of the family of the late A.J. Clarke).

found. The ships' log of *Saint John* gives the location of the U-boat as 58°09'30"N. 02°23'00"W.

Still unable to confirm a successful kill, with morning the *Saint John* commenced her attack once more. At 08.00 on the 17th a ten-charge pattern was dropped, with Hedgehog at 08.15 and five more depth charges at 08.30.[11] This relentless barrage continued the stream of wreckage appearing at the surface. Among the evidence gathered from this attack were pieces of French charts of the Caribbean Sea, corrected to 1943, lumps of cork, small pieces of biscuit and hard tack, and the ever present splintered wood - some of which was enamelled. The map fragment was marked 'Hydrographic Office Kiel Section'. Subsequent charges brought up more oil and a piece of door panel about six feet long with its unrusted hinges still attached.

The attacks continued throughout the 17th, and it was noted that with each barrage of depth charges or Hedgehog, the evidence brought to the surface was getting less and less. In fact by 15.15 hours on the 17th no more conclusive wreckage had been produced.

At this point the *Saint John* carried out another echo sounder trace which showed that the target was in two pieces, and it appeared to the experienced crew that the after section of the U-boat had been completely severed from the main part.[12]

Leading Seaman W. Royds was one of the Asdic operators on board the *Saint John* at the time of the attack. In his memoirs he described the attack thus: "On February 16th we picked up an asdic contact off the Moray Firth, north east of Scotland. It appeared to be a U-boat lying on the bottom. Vern Hoffner was the asdic operator at the time. I joined him as this was my action station. We made several attacks and brought up a lot of debris. We held contact through the night. The Echo Sounder produced a distinctive submarine shape at a depth of about 35 fathoms. In all we dropped about 40 depth charges and several Hedgehog patterns".[13]

In addition to the attacks by *Saint John, Nene* had also made sporadic passes over the contact. At 16.45 on the 17th, two more members of EG.9, the *Monnow* and *Loch Alvie*, arrived and continued to add to the pounding that the target was receiving. As they carried on through the night the *Saint John*, which had disengaged from the attack, made for Scapa Flow. Before leaving she had dipped a bucket tied to the end of a length of rope into the water which was described as being 'flooded with oil'. The oil retrieved with this bucket was found to be enough to fill a large quart bottle.[14] At 18.00 hours, as the ship's log noted that the *Saint John* was steaming for Scapa, the Watch was changed and normality resumed. By 21.00 hours most of the crew were watching a movie in the ship's mess deck![15]

By the morning of the 18th the *Monnow* and *Loch Alvie*, who had held contact throughout this second night, had had enough. Despite having fired off numerous barrages of Squid[16] and depth charges only more oil, plenty of bubbles and a small yellow cylinder (which was not recovered by *Monnow*) were seen on the surface. At 10.00 on the morning of the 18th, they too disengaged, turned and set course for Scapa Flow to join the rest of EG.9.[17]

Peace in this part of the North Sea was short lived. Two days later, on the 20th February 1945, three of the frigates of EG.9 - the *Monnow, Nene* and *Loch Alvie* returned. Once again, and with little difficulty, they located the contact. The position was the same as when they had retired two days previously. Once more they commenced a sporadic attack, bringing up the last vestiges of oil and splintered wood.[18]

Only late on the afternoon of the 20th, certain that whoever the U-boat was it had been destroyed, did the frigates of EG.9 finally abandon their victim for the last time.

To many the attack on U-309 had been an almost perfect text-book action. Lieutenant Commander Doug McLean reflects the feelings of many. In a postwar report he stated that "the skillful way in which U-309 was discovered and dispatched after it reached a favourable position to ambush shipping indicates that EG-9, with its long experience in shallow water, was among the groups that led the way in applying shallow water tactical expertise".[19]

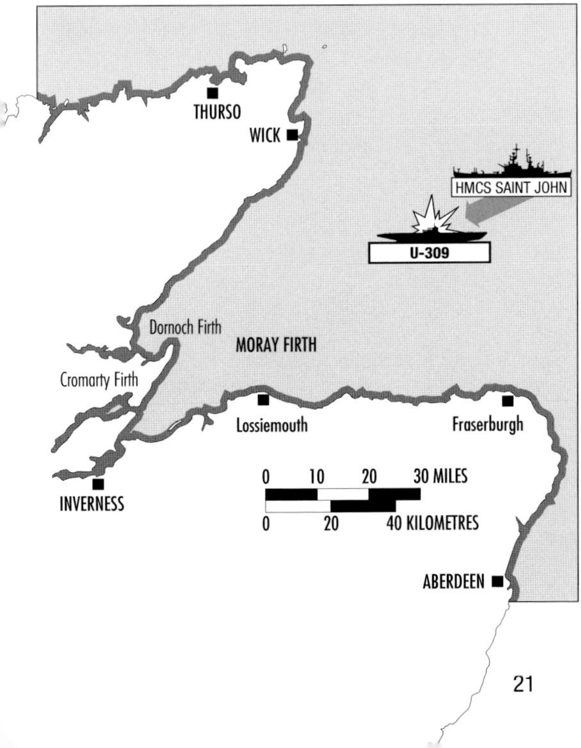

Map showing the location of the sinking of U-309.

In Memoriam

Commander

OL (zs) Herbert Loeder, (03/04/19)

Engineer Officer

Lt (Eng) Hans-Ulrick Winter, (29/10/23)

Watch Officers

OL (zs) Franz-Michael Viehmann, (25/04/21)
Lt (zs) Gunter Drebes, (07/04/21)
Lt (zs) Alfred Kliemstein, (14/03/21)

The Crew

Willi Alberti* (21/02/22)
Herbert Ambrecht* (23/01/24)
Josef Angermair* (04/11/22)
Gerhard Arlt* (11/09/24)
Rolf Auerbach* (15/03/16)
Johann Bauer (19/01/23)
Karl Bohm (18/06/25)
Karl-Heinz Brorsen (16/03/21)
Wilhelm Bruggemann (20/02/25)
Reinhold Cuber (27/08/23)
Ernst Dauben (08/03/25)
Hans Edler (24/11/26)
Kurt Feller* (24/04/20)
Wilhelm Fischer* (16/10/20)
Alois Grommer (12/04/25)
Gerhard Gruschwitz (17/12/22)
Egon Haumann (29/11/22)
Heinz Hylla (27/03/24)
Robert Kaul* (02/10/21)
Rolf Konig (02/10/26)
Siegfried Kunze* (06/07/23)
Alfred Leschniok (07/11/22)
Herbert Lieb (05/11/23)
Hermann Loberenz (17/02/21)
Oskar Lukas (17/06/23)
Peter Mentsches (19/10/24)
Wilhelm Moller* (16/08/15)
Rudolf Neugebauer* (22/08/22)
Friedrich Niethammer (19/08/24)
Heinrich Obst* (26/12/20)
Wilhelm Overmeyer 16/08/24)
Gerhard Oppermann* (23/09/23)
Johann Pesch (09/10/25)
Josef Pikard (08/10/22)
Gunter Schlotmann* (15/06/21)
Fritz Schluter* (25/01/16)
Rudi Schneeberg (17/10/15)
Josef Spyth (08/03/22)
Herbert Stater (16/12/22)
Josef Weis (28/10/24)
Reimund Weitemeyer (01/06/24)
Eduard Winter (31/05/21)

There are no roses on a sailor's grave
No lilies on an ocean wave
The only tribute is the seagull's sweeps
And the teardrops that a sweetheart weeps.

(German Song)

(* Served on board U309 from day of commissioning until lost off Wick)

THE WRECK

Above: Here are the remains of U-309's bow after it was blown apart by the depth charge attacks of 1945, clearly demonstrating the destructive power and ferocity of the continued attack by H.M.C.S. *Saint John.* (Both photographs by kind permission of Petra Lachmann).

Below: This view is of the starboard bow looking forward. It shows the total destruction of the pressure hull and what was the bow compartment and torpedo room of U-309. All that remains now is a pile of twisted and torn metal.

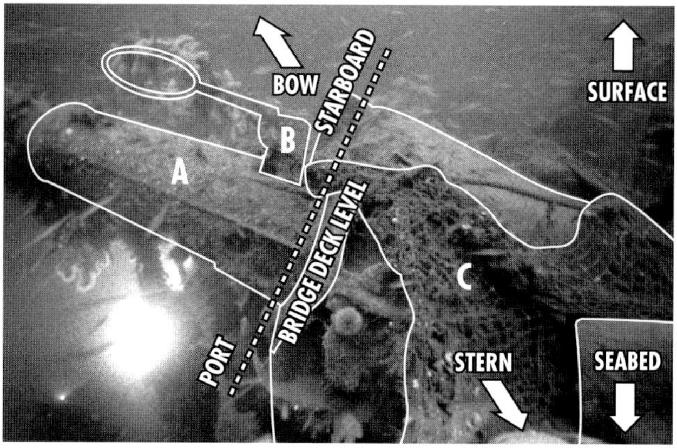

A photograph looking forward from the conning tower just behind the attack periscope housing (A) and showing the loop aerial (B).

Clearly visible in the foreground are tangled trawl nets (C) caught on the wreck. From this photograph you can appreciate the attitude of the wreck as she sits on the sea bed. (By kind permission of Petra Lachmann).

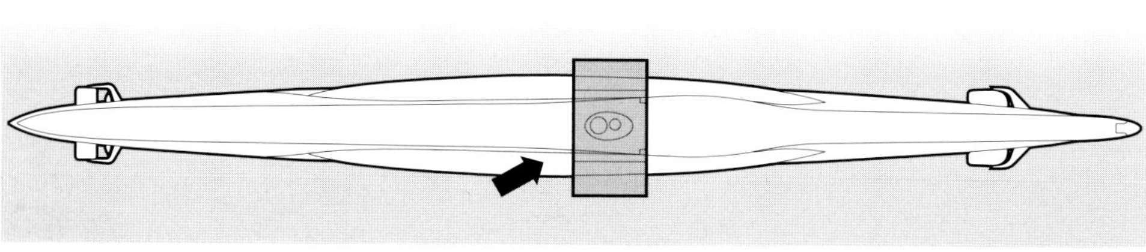

Another view of the conning tower but this time directly from above. From this position you are looking down through an open hatch (A) and into the U-boat itself.

To the left of this photograph can be seen the sky periscope housing (B), the loop aerial (C) and what remains of the snorkel raising assembly (D).
(By kind permission of Petra Lachmann).

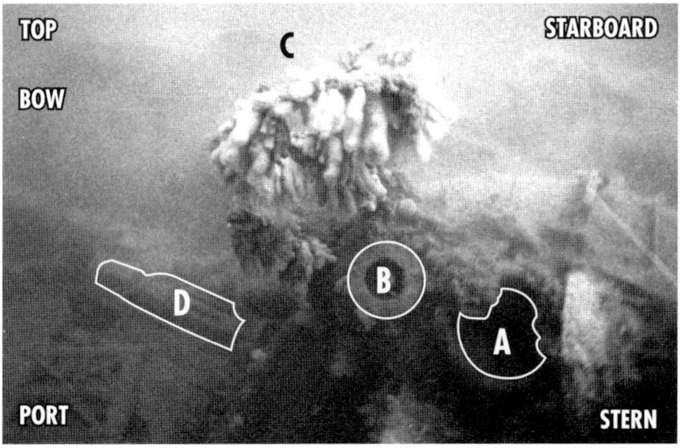

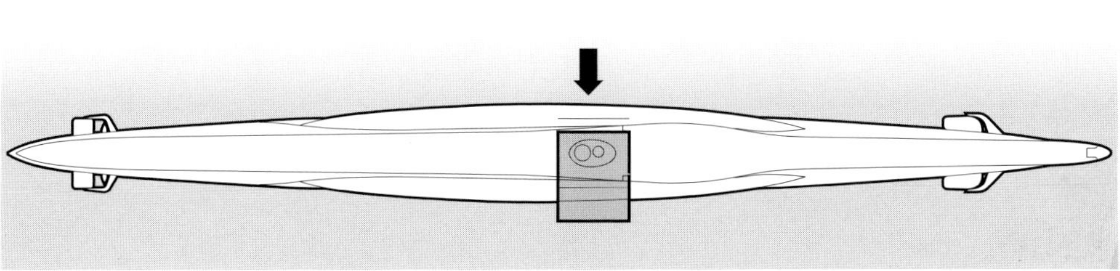

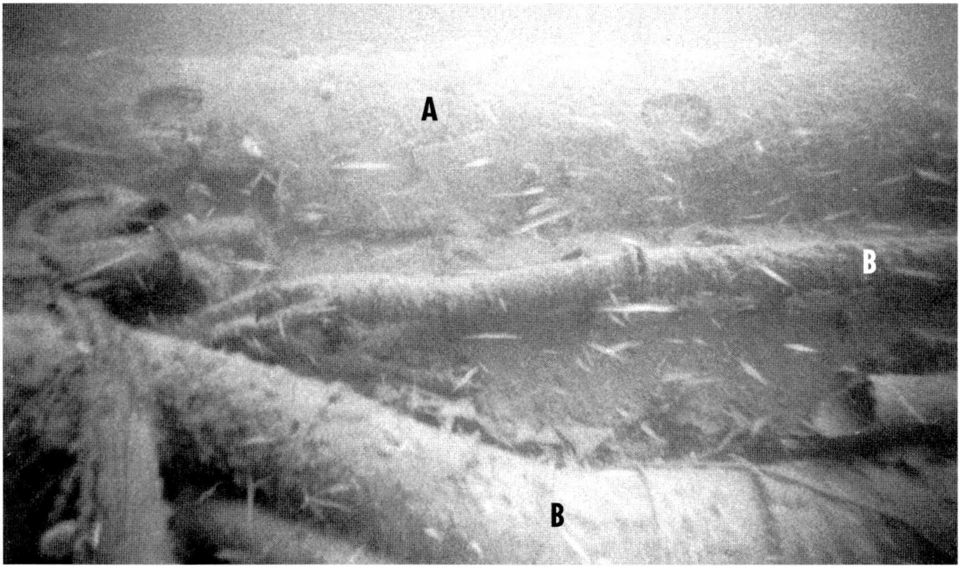

Above: A view of the port saddle tank (A) immediately aft of the conning tower. Normally the extensive pipework and air trunking shown (B) would be hidden below the deck casing, which has been lost either during the attack or eroded with time. (Both photographs by kind permission of Petra Lachmann).

Below: Taken from the port side of the conning tower, to the left can be seen the loop aerial assembly (A) and sky periscope housing (B). Right and aft of the housing can be seen an open access hatch (C) behind which can be seen the attack periscope housing (D).

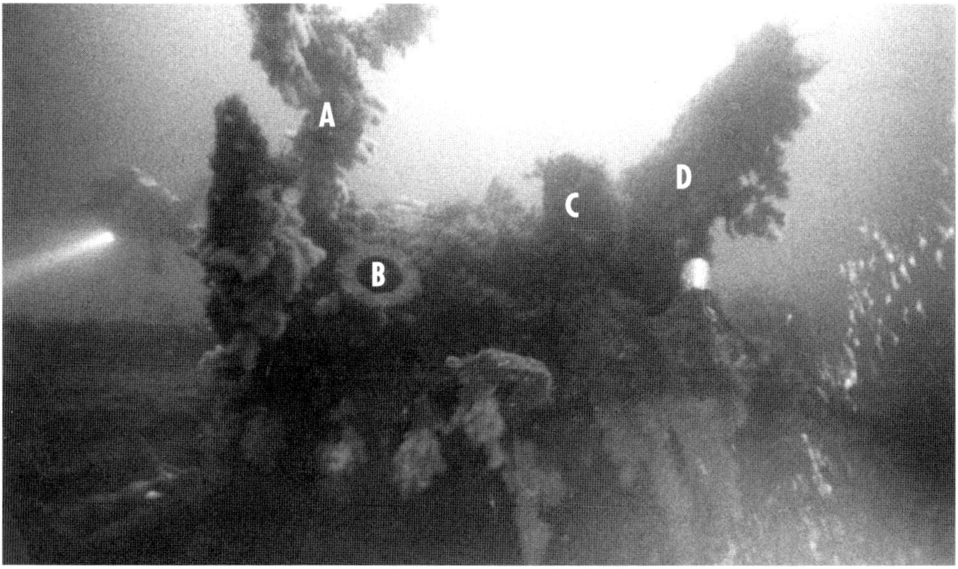

MEDALS AND AWARDS

A graphic representation of H.M.C.S. *Saint John* in action. This painting, by Saint John artist Ray Butler, is an enormous mural on the side of the building owned by the Main Brace Naval Veterans Association. This building can be found on Main Street, Saint John. (By kind permission of Mr. H.E. Wright).

The wreck photographs contained in this book are evidence that the target of EG.9's relentless attacks over the four-day period, U-309, had suffered a terrible fate. It is difficult to imagine that this wreck on the floor of the Moray Firth was once one of the most-feared weapons in Germany's wartime arsenal. This U-boat was lost with all hands, fourteen of whom had served on U-309 from her day of commissioning. Eight were engineering personnel, four were seaman branch and two were radio operators. Unfortunately for these men, U-309 was to be the first U-boat to be sighted in the area for nearly five years.

By the very nature of her fate, nothing was ever heard from U-309 or her crew ever again. As far as the German High Command was concerned everything should have been well. This situation was no doubt compounded by the fact that, by this stage of the war, the German High Command held a suspicion that the allies could monitor radio transmissions and obtain location fixes from messages sent by a U-boat. Commanders were instructed to receive and not transmit messages - unless under extenuating circumstances.

Intercepted and decoded Enigma transmissions show that, unaware of her loss on the 16th February, messages were still being transmitted for the attention of U-309.[1] On the 25th February Loeder was informed that there was "a barrage in naval grid square 05395 which is impassable for submarines". This message went on to state that it was "passed daily by one convoy (inward bound) between 03.00 and 10.00, and outward bound between 12.00 and 16.00". Loeder was instructed that these convoys operated at a speed of 7.5 knots and that he had 'freedom of action' to respond.

High Command continued to issue instructions to U-309. On the 12th March, barely 12 weeks from the end of the war, the

The *Saint John* in dock, believed to be Cardiff, for repairs to damage sustained during the attack on U-309. (By kind permission of The Stacey Collection).

message was clearly one to fight on. Three U-boats, including U-309, were informed: "In your area HECKEL let by many smallish ships - up to 2,000 GRT - with an eye to a better chance. For 7C boats this procedure is wrong. Don't wait long - knock them out as they come". Thirteen days later on the 25th, a terse instruction, addressed to Loeder, simply states "Port of destination is Bergen". Receiving no reply, and possibly with the no show from U-309, on the 10th April 1945 this was followed by another message for Loeder: "Warned not to exhaust your crew".

Interestingly, U-309 was not the only vessel damaged in the attack. The *Saint John* had departed from the scene on the evening of the 17th because she herself had been damaged during the attack. The tremendous number of depth charges and Hedgehogs detonated at slow speeds by the crew of *Saint John* had caused flooding in a number of her compartments. In his diary, Able Seaman A.J. 'Knobby' Clarke, describes the damage suffered by the *Saint John*. On the 18th February, (having arrived at Scapa at 21.00 the previous evening), he wrote "slipped at 08.15 and tied up alongside *Vindictive* to get hull inspection. Inspected by Harbour Master and [he] claims that we are not seaworthy. Taking in 1,000 tons of water a day. Looks like the slips somewhere as they can't do the job here - Liverpool I hope."[2]

On arrival at Scapa Flow, naval divers had indeed confirmed the extent of the damage suffered by the frigate. No longer fit for front line service, instructions were issued for her return to Canada. Prior to setting out across the Atlantic she docked at Cardiff, permitting temporary repairs to be carried out over the next six weeks, before onward travel to Saint John, New Brunswick.[3] These repairs had not been completed by the time the war in

Above: Commander Arthur Frank Capel Layard R.N., Senior officer of the 9th Escort Group. (By kind permission of the family of the late A.J. Clarke).

Below: The ship's crest of H.M.C.S. *Saint John*. (By kind permission of the family of the late Cable Freeman).

Europe ended, and so the *Saint John* was placed in reserve in November 1945, and finally scrapped in 1947.[4]

Despite the evidence plucked from the water and the extent of the barrage rained down upon the target, the *Saint John* was not initially awarded a confirmed 'kill'. In a report dated the 28th May 1945, C.D. Howard-Johnston, the Director of the Anti U-boat Division, noted "it is confirmed that the action has been assessed U-boat probably sunk".[5] Those onboard the *Saint John* did not hold any such doubts. One narrative states that Able Seaman Joe McLaren was so certain that the target was a 'dead duck' that he painted a second submarine silhouette on the forward 4" gun shield. McLaren had been one of those seamen sent out in the whaler to gather the necessary evidence of a kill. He recalled attempting to rip an eagle and swastika emblem from a jacket that he had pulled inboard while still attempting to row.[6] His fellow crew member Able Seaman Cable Freeman, an Asdic operator, was so certain that in his diary entry for the 17th February 1945 he recorded an almost identical conclusion: "U-boat dead duck... this is our second German U-boat kill".[7]

These inconclusive official findings had been outlined in an earlier report, this time dated the 30th April 1945.[8] The 'probable' assessment was reached despite the fact that, in this report, the Commanding Officer's opinion was clearly stated: "It is considered that the U-boat was killed as even the strongest hull possible could not have withstood the continuous heavy and accurate bombardment with depth charges and Hedgehog".

In due course a number of the crew of the *Saint John* were recommended for honours or awards. In recommending Acting Commander Arthur Frank Capel Layard a D.S.C.[9] the following was noted. "This attack was conducted in an accurate and masterful

The Asdic crew of H.M.C.S. *Saint John*, pictured at Halifax in April 1943. Back row, left to right are:- Leading Seaman Ray Kopetiuk; Able Seaman Wally Thomas; Able Seaman Pearse and Able Seaman Norman 'Vern' Hoffner D.S.M., and unknown. The two in the front are Able Seaman Cable Freeman and Leading Seaman William Royds D.S.M. (By kind permission of the family of the late Cable Freeman).

manner, and throughout a period of almost twenty four hours, Commander Layard displayed ability, good judgement and perseverance. Under his direction the *Saint John* dropped a total of 65 depth charges and 6 patterns of Hedgehog, which produced oil and splintered wood". The report went on to state that "Layard has been Senior Officer of the 9th Escort Group for a year and has carried out much useful support work". [10]

Layard was not the only member of *Saint John's* crew to be rewarded. Lieutenant James Bradley, who had been the Officer of the Watch when U-309 was first discovered, gained a bar to his Distinguished Service Cross. D.S.M.s were awarded to Engine Room Artificer 2nd Class Thomas Whittemore, Leading Seaman Leslie Stannard, and Able Seaman Norman Hoffner. Lieutenant Charles George McIntosh, under whose temporary command the *Saint John* had been operating, was to be Mentioned In Dispatches, as were Stoker Petty Officer Albert Seymour, A/Leading Stoker George Styles, and Able Seaman John Hammond.[11]

Two ratings, Petty Officer D.L. King and Able Seaman J. Miller, were subsequently given Commander-In-Chief's Commendations. It also appears that the Office of Commodore Destroyers had recommended that another officer, Lieutenant N. Earl, receive a Mention In Dispatches, but this was, for whatever reason, not ratified by the Chairman of the Honours and Awards Committee.[12] The final award to be made was a D.S.M. for Leading Seaman William Royds. Royds had manned the Asdic as First Operator for the majority of the attacks, although it must be pointed out that this award had originated in the work he had also carried out on the earlier attack on U-247.[13]

Whilst only a fraction of the crew of *Saint John* were officially recognised for the sinking of U-309, there can be no doubt that it had been a team effort. Leading Seaman William 'Bill' Royds later wrote on this matter. "The Coxswain, Warburton, the ERAs and Stokers, the Gunners, Tels and Coders, the Signallers, the Stewards, the ASDIC and 'Huff Duff' operators, the LTOs, the Cooks and Sick Bay 'Tiffies' and, of course, the indispensable ODs, ABs, Killocks, Petty Officers and Chiefs - above or below deck. These are the ones who made the ship the fighting force that it was. And this is true on all our vessels. The Commander got the glory and in most cases, well deserved glory, but it was the whole team working as a unit that made our ship successful in spite of bad weather, bad living conditions and lack of sleep!"[14]

With Post-war assessments of German naval records confirming what the Commander and crew of H.M.C.S. *Saint John* had always known, the destruction of U-309 and the loss of Loeder and his crew leaves us with one question that will always remain unknown. Did the first meeting between *Saint John* and U-309 take place on the 16th, or had the *Saint John* in fact stumbled across her before?

Despite being the youngest seaman aboard the *Saint John*, Able Seaman Cable Freeman kept a detailed diary of his time aboard ship. Freeman is fondly remembered by many of his shipmates, such as the likes of Bill Royds. Royds remembers an occasion when

Some of the crew of H.M.C.S. *Saint John*. Back from left to right:- unknown, Kopetiuk, Hoffner and Freeman. Front:- Thomas, unknown, and Royds. (By kind permission of the family of the late Lt. Cmdr. Stacey).

The ship's bell of H.M.C.S. *Saint John*, which having been presented to the city of that name in 1947, can still be seen in its museum, along with the last White Ensign flown by the *Saint John*. A file of H.M.C.S. *Saint John* is now held by Heritage Resources, Saint John, and contains not only the material uncovered during the research for this book, but also H.M.C.S. *Saint John's* commissioning pennant and the White Ensign flown by her on D-Day. (By kind permission of Mr. H.E. Wright).

Freeman, despite his age, had pretended to be an officer one Christmas Day. Royds wrote that Freeman, "cavorting away... with a certain degree of intoxication", had succeeded in being served at the Officer's Club in Derry.[15]

In his diary entry for the 11th February 1945, Freeman describes an encounter with a suspected U-boat. "At sea. Sweeping arch between Shetland Islands and Orkneys. U-boat reported by aircraft in area. 10.55 hours - Action Stations. Contact of U-boat picked up. Fired 2 H/H [Hedgehog] patterns. U-boat deep. Asdic conditions fair. Escort Group 10 sweeping south. 2300 hours - lost contact." [16]

Equally, during the early hours of Thursday the 15th February 1945, the log of H.M.C.S. *Saint John* tells us that once again the frigate was in action.[17] At 02.20 hours another EG.9 frigate, the *Monnow*, reported a contact and requested assistance from the *Saint John*. The *Saint John* made a number of echo soundings, and at 04.02 also located the contact. After circling the contact for over three hours and convinced that a possible U-boat had been located, the order to attack was given, and a pattern of ten depth charges dropped. With no visible results, the attack was abandoned two hours later at 10.02 hours. From the log, we can see that the attack took place roughly 25 miles from where U-309 was sunk the next day. Could it be that the *Saint John* had stumbled across the U-309, only for it to escape, move away and be rediscovered and sunk the very next day?

FOOTNOTES

U-309

1. The extracts from reports containing information on the activity of U-309 can be found in three separate files stored at the Public Record Office, (PRO), in Kew. These files have the references HW 18/350; HW 18/377 and HW 18/ 406.
2. PRO HW 18/350, page 118.
3. PRO HW 18/377, page 64.
4. Engine Room Artificer Kurt Feller, born on the 24th April 1920, had been a member of the crew on U-309 from the date of commissioning. He was one of those lost when U-309 was sunk. It is not recorded whether Feller ever got the opportunity to see his son.
5. The *S.S. Samneva* was a Liberty Ship built at Los Angeles by the Californian Shipbuilding Corporation Inc. and launched in September 1943 as the *Henry M. Stanley*. She was immediately transferred to Britain under the Lend-Lease agreements, renamed the *Samneva*, and operated by A. Holt & Co. of Liverpool. It is worth noting that all Liberty ships supplied to the United Kingdom, (with one exception), were given names prefixed with the letters SAM. This indicated that the vessel had the 'superstructure aft of midships'. No casualties were suffered as a result of the attack by U-309, and she was able to limp to Southampton where, in immediate danger of sinking, she was beached. Classified as a constructive total loss, the *Samneva* remained here until 1947, at which point the stern section was salved and subsequently scrapped, leaving the fore part to be scrapped in situ.